A SPIRITUAL HISTORY
OF THE ROYAL MILE

BY PAUL JAMES-GRIFFITHS

The writer Tobias Smollett once said: *'Edinburgh is a hot bed of genius.'* And the centre of that hotbed is the Royal Mile (High Street) and its side-streets. Stretching for a mile from the Castle at the top to the Holyrood Palace at the bottom, this street has impacted the world in a way that is truly extraordinary. Indeed, it has been a hotbed of spirituality and philosophy that has shaped the globe.

Latent Publishing

Latent Publishing

Copyright © 2008 Paul James-Griffiths

First published September 2008 by Latent Publishing

Latent Publishing is an imprint of Latent Publishing Ltd.

Latent Publishing Ltd.
P.O. Box 23919
Pathhead, Scotland
EH37 5YG

www.latentpublishing.com

The right of Paul James-Griffiths to be identified as the author
of this work has been asserted by him in accordance with the
Copyright, Designs and Patents Act 1988.

British Library Cataloguing in Publication Data

A catalogue record for this book is available from the British Library.

ISBN 0-9548821-2-1

Printed and bound in Great Britain.

Website: theroyalmile.org.uk

A project of **Edinburgh City Mission**

E l info@ecm.org.uk **T l** 0131 554 6140
A l 9 Pilrig Street, Edinburgh, EH6 5AH **W l** www.ecm.org.uk
A Charity registered in Scotland No.SC 012385

Design: Miriam McWilliam **W l** www.boxroomcollective.com **E l** miriam@mcwilliam.id.au
Photography: Miriam McWilliam and Paul James-Griffiths.

CONTENTS

IMAGE: A view from the Edinburgh Castle. Photograph: Miriam McWilliam

IMAGE: The witchcraft memorial fountain on the Castle esplanade. Photograph: Miriam McWilliam

THE CULDEES: THE CELTIC PERIOD

EARLIEST TIMES

Long ago volcanic activity caused seven hills to emerge in an area in Scotland which became known as Dyn Eiddyn. Castle Hill became ideal as a stronghold for people and was fought over continually by the pagans who lived there. The Picts, Scots, the Welsh-speaking Britons, known to the Romans as Votadini (Goddodin), the Angles (English) Romans and French all had a part in moulding the character of the city that eventually grew up here.

In the Bronze Age the people worshipped created things like the sun, moon and stars, and they had many gods. Indeed, Edinburgh is in the heart of the area known as the Lothians, or Lleuthern, meaning the fortress of Lleu, who was the sun god.

THE COMING OF THE CHRISTIANS

In about AD 200 Tertullian wrote that Christians had spread even into the most northern areas of Britain.[1] It is possible that the first Christians who may have come to Edinburgh were Roman soldiers; certainly there were Roman barracks in Cramond dating from AD 140, and even a Roman boathouse dating from the first century AD. By AD 397 Ninian had built a stone church north of Hadrian's Wall and Christianity was spreading in Scotland. He also appears to have set up a mission base at Abercorn, about 12 miles from Edinburgh. Waves of missionaries started pouring in to reach the Celts, Picts and Scots.

The Roman, Palladius, was appointed as a bishop missionary to the people in AD 423, and according to the historical information at Culross Abbey, he arrived in Culross in AD 424 to find that Serf had already established a monastery at that site (in Fife, on the other side of the Forth estuary).

According to a strong tradition, Princess Denw (Thenew) was driven away from her people by her father, King Lleuddon (Loth), because she was found with child out of wedlock. There are two stories concerning her: either she conceived through fornication, or she was a Christian who was raped and became pregnant. The people tried to kill her by throwing her off the Traprain Law (a hill-rock outside Edinburgh, near Haddington) but she miraculously survived. She was put in a coracle and left to drift out to sea, where she eventually arrived at Culross.

The monks there looked after her and she gave birth to Kentigern (Mungo), who eventually became the apostle of the Strathclyde district and Bishop of Cumbria in AD 543. He established the Church in Glasgow but preached all the way from Galloway to the Orkneys in the far north. Glasgow itself was founded by him and the name *Glas-gu* means 'dear family'. The city motto there is: *Lord, let Glasgow flourish through the preaching of thy Word and the praise of thy name.* Such are the amazing redemptive purposes of God.

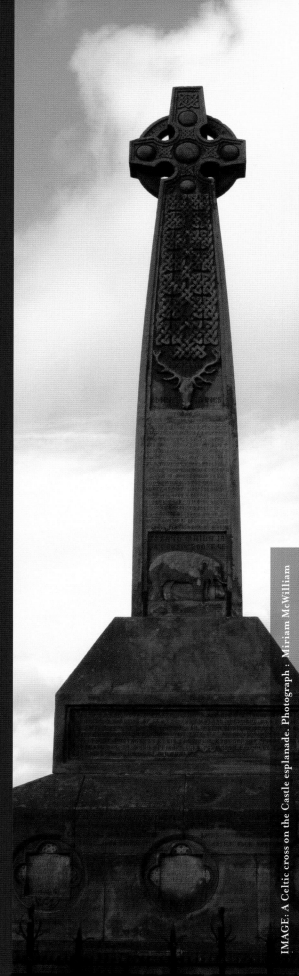

IMAGE: A Celtic cross on the Castle esplanade. Photograph: Miriam McWilliam

KING ARTHUR

If you walk to the bottom of the Royal Mile next to the Scottish Parliament you cannot miss the rugged hill that towers over Edinburgh, with Arthur's Seat perched on top. It stands like a sentinel; if only rocks could tell us the history of mankind! For many people, King Arthur is a mysterious, legendary figure from the murky past. Nobody seems to know how and when Arthur's Seat received its name. Legend has it that King Arthur himself was there, but there is no historical proof of this. However, there are a few historical threads that point to this legend having some truth.

Professor Francis Nigel Lee, who holds the extraordinary honour of having eleven earned Ph.D.s, wrote an article about King Arthur, in which he says:

> 'Arthur was the Christian "High King" or Arh-an-Rhaig of the Britons. Several have attempted to locate him at Gelliwig alias Kelliwic in Cornwall, where he may indeed have had at least a summer palace in his large western domain (comprising the better part of Brythonic Britain all the way from Dumbarton in the north to Land's End in the south... It seems very clear from authentic records, that the Christian King Arthur really did fight twelve major battles against the non-Christian Saxons But there is more. Precisely the localities of those battles, tends to centre not in Cornwall but in Cumbria in the Northwest; (in) Southern Scotland; and (in) the ancient kingdom of Rheged around the Solway. Cat Coit Celidon, the Battle of the Caledonian Forest, is unequivocally Northern — and is usually taken to refer to the wooded country north of Carlisle.' [2]

The Elizabethan chronicler, Raphael Holinshed, drawing from early historical sources, says that Arthur was crowned King of the Britons in AD 516, and that he made an alliance with King Loth of the Picts, who ruled the Lothians and was St Kentigern's grandfather. If this is true, then the large rock at the bottom of the Royal Mile may indeed have witnessed King Arthur, as wooden fortresses were built on such high places in the Edinburgh area, and Arthur's Seat may have been a military stronghold for this alliance against the Saxons.

COLUMBA AND IONA

An Irish aristocrat, named Columba, came with a team of monks to reach the Picts in AD 563 and they set up their mission base on the island of Iona near Mull on the west coast. One of their communities was at Dunkeld, about two days' walk from Edinburgh and so it is likely that the Church already existed here by then.

Those early Celtic Christians became known as Culdees (from the Gaelic *Celi De* — 'friends of God'), since it was obvious to all the pagans that these people really knew Christ because of their humility, practical loving care and answers to prayer. Many are the accounts of miracles occurring through Columba.

IMAGE: A stained glass Columba in St Margaret's Chapel, Edinburgh Castle. Photograph: Paul James-Griffiths

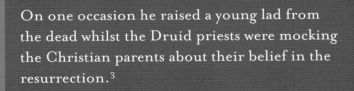

On one occasion he raised a young lad from the dead whilst the Druid priests were mocking the Christian parents about their belief in the resurrection.[3]

Another time Columba was getting ready to sail across Loch Ness to preach, when a leading pagan priest called Briochan tried to stop him by calling on his gods to send a thick mist and an unfavourable wind. His prayers were answered and the wind and fog came, but Columba calmly stepped into the loch and prayed for the fog to clear and for the wind to change, which happened straightaway, much to the shock of the pagans![4] It is not surprising that multitudes of pagans turned to Christ and left their gods when they saw such a demonstration of love and spiritual power.

Those early Celtic Christians pioneered centres that were truly holistic and founded on Christ. Counselling, healing, education, the arts, agriculture, prayer and mission were important elements of community life.

AIDAN AND HOLY ISLAND (Lindisfarne)

King Oswald had become a Christian as a child whilst staying as a refugee with the community at Iona. As a grown man he re-conquered his family's land and lived in Bamburgh Castle on the Northumbrian coast. He requested that missionaries be sent to Northumbria, which was a district stretching right up to Edinburgh. A team was sent, led by Corman, but returned dejected and defeated, claiming that the Northumbrians were too hard-hearted.

Instead, Aidan was sent with a team and King Oswald gave them Holy Island (Lindisfarne) as their base. Aidan, an Irish man, could not understand English, so King Oswald acted as his interpreter on their preaching tours!

In AD 638 King Oswald drove out the Goddodin from Dyn Eiddyn and it is thought by some that he renamed the town Edwinesburg, after his Christian uncle, King Edwin. Thus we may arrive at the name Edinburgh. However, the name Edinburgh may just be the Anglo-Saxon version of the Celtic Dyn Eiddyn ('burgh' is the Anglo-Saxon word for the Celtic 'dun', both of which mean 'district').

CUTHBERT

The patron saint of Northumbria is Cuthbert, who was born near the River Tweed in AD 635. This district included Edinburgh until 1237. Our historical source of information about this saint comes from Bede 29 years after Cuthbert's death.

Bede says:

> *'I have written nothing about the saint without first subjecting the facts to the most thorough scrutiny and have passed on nothing to be transcribed for general reading that has not been obtained by rigorous examination of trustworthy witnesses.'* [5]

IMAGE: Above: Statue of Cuthbert on Holy Island (Lindisfarne) Below: 'Cuthbert' as a modern-day guide for the Celtic Tour. Photographs: Paul James-Griffiths

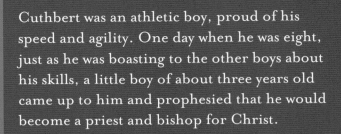

Cuthbert was an athletic boy, proud of his speed and agility. One day when he was eight, just as he was boasting to the other boys about his skills, a little boy of about three years old came up to him and prophesied that he would become a priest and bishop for Christ.

A few years later the household servants put him outside on a stretcher for fresh air because he could not walk on account of a terrible knee tumour. A stranger appeared in white on horseback and told him to make a poultice of warm milk and wheaten flour and put it on his knee; then he rode off. Cuthbert did so and was healed within a few days.

God called Cuthbert to be a monk at the age of 16 on 31st August, AD 651. He was looking after a flock of sheep at night when he saw light streaming from heaven and angelic choirs coming down to earth to take the soul of a holy man to be with Christ. He woke the other shepherds and told them what he had seen and that God had called him to leave his job and become a monk at Melrose Abbey. He found out later that the soul he had seen ascending to heaven was that of Aidan, founder of the community at Holy Island, or Lindisfarne, who had died that night. In his last few years Cuthbert did indeed become the bishop of the community at Holy Island, in accordance with the boy's prediction.

MIRACLES AND HEALINGS

Often God would supply his needs supernaturally, and animals such as an eagle would be sent to provide food. He would pray through the night, sometimes with his body in the sea up to the neck to keep awake, and when he came out sea otters would rush over to him and lie on him to keep him warm.

Many people were healed through Cuthbert's prayers. A paralysed boy was brought to him who was healed instantly. Cuthbert *'had recourse to his usual armoury, prayer, gave a blessing and drove away the disease for which the doctors, despite their skill in concocting medicines, had been unable to devise a cure. The youth regained his strength, stood up and gave thanks to God, and went back home with the women who had brought him.'* [6]

In fact, so many were being healed that people travelled many miles to cross over to Holy Island and receive prayer and counsel:

> *'Now Cuthbert had great numbers of people coming to him not just from Lindisfarne but even from the remote parts of Britain, attracted by his reputation for miracles. They confessed their sins, confided in him about their temptations, and laid open to him the common troubles of humanity they were labouring under — all in the hope of gaining consolation from so holy a man They were not disappointed. No one left unconsoled, no one had to carry back the burdens he came with.*
>
> *Spirits that were chilled with sadness he could warm back to hope again with a pious word. Those beset with worry he brought back to thoughts of the joys of heaven.*

THE PARISH OF ST. CUTHBERT

ACCORDING TO TRADITION, CHRISTIAN WORSHIP HAS BEEN CELEBRATED CONTINUOUSLY ON THIS SITE FOR THIRTEEN CENTURIES. SEVERAL CHURCHES HAVE STOOD HERE, BELOW THE CASTLE ROCK, INCLUDING, IT IS SAID, ONE FOUNDED BY ST. CUTHBERT HIMSELF. THE STEEPLE OF THE PRESENT PARISH CHURCH DATES FROM 1789. THE REST OF THE CHURCH WAS COMPLETED IN 1894. AMONG THE NOTABLE PEOPLE BURIED IN THE CHURCHYARD ARE JOHN NAPIER, INVENTOR OF LOGARITHMS, AND THOMAS DE QUINCEY, WRITER.

IMAGE: Above: The Parish of St Cuthbert plaque. Photograph: Paul James-Griffiths. Below: Cobblestones on the Royal Mile. Photograph: Miriam McWilliam

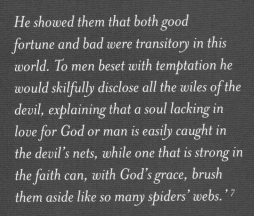

*He showed them that both good
fortune and bad were transitory in this
world. To men beset with temptation he
would skilfully disclose all the wiles of the
devil, explaining that a soul lacking in
love for God or man is easily caught in
the devil's nets, while one that is strong in
the faith can, with God's grace, brush
them aside like so many spiders' webs.'* [7]

ANGELS AND DEMONS

Cuthbert was often refreshed by God's angels
in his labours of love to the people. Bede tells
us: *'Angels would often appear and talk with him and
when he was hungry he would be refreshed with food by
the special gift of God.'* [8]

However, he also encountered evil spirits
who opposed his message. A group of
windswept islands called Inner Farne off
the Northumbrian coast became his prayer
sanctuary. The locals had warned him of the
ghosts that haunted the place and *'Cuthbert was
the first man brave enough to live there alone.'* [9]

Instead of finding human ghosts there,
Cuthbert found poltergeist demons which
he drove away through prayer and fasting in
Christ's name. He said:

*'How often have the demons tried to cast me
headlong from yonder rock; how often have
they hurled stones as if to kill me; with one fantastic
temptation after another they have sought to
disillusion me into retreating from this battlefield; but
they have never yet succeeded in harming either soul
or body; nor do they terrify me.'* [10]

IMAGE: Dark versus light. Photograph: Miriam McWilliam

Once, when he was preaching to a crowd in a village about the dangers of Satan's temptations, a phantom fire came and rested on a house. The locals tried to put out the flames, but because it was a spiritual fire from the devil, nothing was burning up.

Cuthbert rebuked the evil one and he left. Then he turned to the stunned people and said: *'In these days of darkness what we need is a fire from the North.'* He meant that we need to turn away from all sin, wrongdoing, witchcraft and idolatry in its many forms, and find the true supernatural in God through Jesus Christ alone.

I wonder what he would have made of Edinburgh's 'underground city' today, with all its reports of 'ghosts' and 'poltergeists'?

EDINBURGH

There was a Lothian mission in and around Edinburgh from about AD 650 onwards, and Cuthbert is likely to have been part of this with his friend, Bishop Trumwine of Abercorn (near Edinburgh). There is a strong tradition that Cuthbert used to preach in the market place below what is now Edinburgh Castle, where he built himself a stone hut. Cuthbert died on Inner Farne in AD 687.

IMAGE: Edinburgh Castle, view from Princes St. Photograph: Miriam McWilliam

THE PEARL OF SCOTLAND: THE MIDDLE AGES

If you go to Edinburgh Castle today you will find *The Stone of Destiny*, which is a large stone symbolising Scotland's pride and honour. A lot of mystery surrounds this stone and thousands of Scots have bled and died over it.

Legend has it that the Scythians brought it to Ireland from the Middle East, and then the Scots there (named after Queen Scota) came with it to Argyll when Fergus was crowned first King of the Scots in this nation in AD 498. The tradition was that wherever the Stone was found the Scots would reign supreme and the ancient kings were crowned on it. For a time the Stone was at Iona where Columba anointed kings over it.

In AD 839, Kenneth McAlpine, King of the Scots, ordered the Stone of Destiny to be taken from Argyll and placed at Scone where Scottish kings would be crowned. At this point it became known as *The Stone of Scone*.

In 1296, King Edward I ('Longshanks') stole it from the Scots and took it to Westminster Abbey in London, where it became known as *The Coronation Stone* upon which the kings and queens of England have been crowned. In 1996, the British Prime Minister, John Major, returned it to Edinburgh, where it remains today in the Castle.[11]

Another name for it has been *Jacob's Pillow*. Some people believe it is the original stone 'pillow' upon which Jacob in the Bible (Genesis 28:10-22) slept and had a dream about angels

ascending and descending on a
ladder to heaven. When he awoke
from his dream he named the place
Bethel, meaning 'House of God', and
said: *'this is the gate of heaven'*.

Later Jesus referred to himself as
the spiritual gate through which we
must go to find God (Matthew 7:13)
and said about himself: *'I tell you the
truth, you shall see heaven open, and the
angels of God ascending and descending on
the Son of Man'* (John 1:51). For many
Christians, then, Edinburgh has a
godly purpose in making known the
message of Jesus Christ to all nations.

QUEEN MARGARET (1047–1093)

If you go up to the Castle you will
find that most of the construction is
from the 1450s onwards; very little
exists before that, due to the ravages
of war. One exception is St Margaret's
Chapel, which was built in King
David's time in 1124 and based on a
simpler prayer room that belonged to
his mother, Queen Margaret.

Queen Margaret was an amazing
woman. The Scots loved her and
called her *The Pearl of Scotland* because
of her selfless devotion to God on the
behalf of the poor and needy. She
was married to King Malcolm III,
the successor of King Macbeth (made
famous by Shakespeare) after coming
to Scotland as a refugee when she fled
from William the Conqueror.

IMAGE: St Margaret in her own chapel, Edinburgh Castle. Photograph: Paul James–Griffiths

Her motto was *'To give our Lord perfect service, Martha and Mary must combine.'* This meant that she believed our spiritual lives for Christ must be outworked in practical help and good works.

Her acts of charity and humility were numerous: washing the feet of the poor; feeding the poor and needy in the Castle — she even fed the orphans with her own silver spoon; paying for the rebuilding of the monastery at Iona, which had been ravaged by the Vikings; building new monasteries for the spreading of the gospel of Christ and for use as education and hospital centres. She was also responsible for making Sunday an official day of rest, and she had a ferry established to ship pilgrims across the Forth estuary on their way to St Andrews. Queensferry is named after her today, as is Queen Margaret University.

Her husband was devoted to her. He was illiterate but used to kiss her Bible fondly, believing that somehow he could get closer to the holy presence of God he often felt in this woman of prayer. Sadly he was killed together with their eldest son in a battle at Alnwick. She was already dying when the news arrived, but this heartbreak accelerated her death. She became known as the patron saint of wives, families and the poor, and she used to say to her children:

'If you love Him (i.e. Jesus Christ), my darlings, He will give you prosperity in this life and everlasting happiness with all the saints.'

IMAGE: The Witchery pub. Photograph: Miriam McWilliam

KING DAVID
(RULED FROM 1124–1153)

King David came to the throne in 1124. He followed the faith of his mother and had St Giles' Cathedral built in that time by the Lazarite monks. (A more simple church had probably existed on that site since 854, which had been built by the Benedictine monks.)

The Cathedral itself was named after St Giles, the patron saint of lepers, and the Lazarite monks who cared for the lepers, were named after Lazarus whom Jesus raised from the dead. So here in the heart of Edinburgh is God's symbol of healing from all that is unclean in our lives, and a sign of his resurrection power.

One day King David was hunting in the forest by Arthur's Seat when a stag caused his horse to rear up and he fell to the ground. When he looked up, the stag was about to gore him. He grabbed the stag's antlers and saw a cross shining between the horns.

The stag left him and David went home wondering over this event. That night he had a dream. Three times in this dream he was told to build an abbey at the spot where he saw the cross. He obeyed the dream and so *Holyrood Abbey* (Holyrood means 'Holy Cross') was built, the ruins of which can still be seen next to Holyrood Palace at the bottom of the Royal Mile.

IMAGE: King David's vision of the stag commemorated at Canongate Kirk. Photograph: Miriam McWilliam

A SPIRITUAL VOLCANO: THE REFORMATION

In the Middle Ages the Church, on the whole, became increasingly corrupt and compromised, with pagan ideas permeating it. Godly scholars and monks began to challenge the system of the day and call for a return to biblical Christianity. John Wycliffe, the scholar martyr (1320–1384) from Oxford University triggered a movement that proclaimed freedom of conscience and a direct faith before God without religious trappings. He translated the Bible into English for the common folk and trained preachers to spread the message of Christ. They were nicknamed 'the Lollards'. Some of them came up into Scotland but were martyred, such as James Resby of Perth (1407) and Paul Crawer of St Andrews (1431).

Wycliffe's written works reached Bohemia (Czech Republic) where John Hus (1374–1415) studied them at the University of Prague. He spoke up, and was burnt at the stake. But the preaching spread through Europe and reached the ears of a German monk and Professor, Martin Luther. In 1517 he nailed his famous 95 theses on the door of Wittenberg Cathedral and the Reformation was born.

THE SCOTTISH REFORMATION

Patrick Hamilton, an abbot from a monastery, had been converted in Germany, and he returned to Britain and began preaching in Scotland. He was burnt at the stake at St Andrews Castle in 1528.

With calm assurance he spoke of the forgiveness of sins and eternal life through Christ alone. At his execution he cried out: *'Lord Jesus, receive my spirit! How long shall darkness overwhelm this Realm? How long wilt thou suffer this tyranny of men?'* [12]

Hamilton's death triggered a breakthrough amongst some of the monks called Greyfriars (Franciscans) and Blackfriars (Dominicans) who loved Christ: *'within a few years thereafter, began both Black and Grey Friars publicly to preach against the pride and idle life of the Bishops, and against the abuses of the whole Ecclesiastical Estate.'* [13]

But it was not only the friars and abbots who began to preach on righteousness and expose sin, but Professors at St Andrews University, too. And there was a price to pay, with the martyrdoms of many monks. In 1534 David Stratton and Norman Gourlay were hanged and burnt at Greenside on Calton Hill in Edinburgh. On 28th February, 1538, six more were executed by burning just outside Edinburgh Castle. Their 'crime' had been to preach the message of God through a Passion Play on the Life of Christ, which had a huge impact on the mostly illiterate population.

JOHN KNOX (1514–1572)

'The one Scotchman to whom of all others, his country and the world owe a debt.'
(Thomas Carlyle in 1840)

IMAGE: Statue of John Knox in St Giles' Cathedral. Photograph: Miriam McWilliam

Born near Haddington, just outside Edinburgh, John Knox was ordained as a priest and became a private tutor. He came across the preaching of the Reformers, which began to challenge his thinking. In Scotland the English Bible had been banned and *'The town of Edinburgh, for the most part, was drowned in superstition.'* [14]

Knox was impressed by the preaching of George Wishart, who came to Scotland in 1544, and he decided to become his bodyguard, standing in front of the pulpit with his double-handed sword! Two years later Wishart was burnt at the stake at St Andrews Castle. In 1547 a band of men besieged and took St Andrews Castle and Knox was made preacher. It was said of him:

'Others lopped the branches of the papistry, but he strikes at the root, to destroy the whole.' [15]

The Castle was captured by the French and Knox ended up as a galley slave aboard a French vessel. One day, whilst the ship was just off St Andrews, the fellow slaves passed around a picture of the Virgin Mary to kiss in worship, but he threw it overboard and exclaimed:
'She's light enough; let her learn to swim.'

In 1549 the English ransomed Knox from the French and he ended up preaching before the King of England, the Protestant King Edward VI. When the King died his half-sister, Mary Tudor, came to power in 1553 and Knox wisely fled to Europe, just before Mary went on a rampage, executing hundreds of Protestants, including the four English bishops, Cranmer, Latimer, Ridley and Hooper.

For a short time Knox was in Frankfurt, Germany, before settling in Geneva in Switzerland. This city was the centre of the

Reformation at that time, and he learnt much from its leader, John Calvin.

He wrote that Geneva was:

'the most perfect school of Christ that ever was on earth since the days of the Apostles' and *'the most godly reformed church and city of the world.'* [16]

Whilst Knox was in Geneva, Mary Tudor married Philip II and brought England back under the rule of the Pope. King James V of Scotland was married to Mary de Guise of France and they had a daughter, Mary (Queen of the Scots). Six days after her birth her father died. She had been betrothed to the heir of the English throne, but a French–Scottish government had broken the agreement, which resulted in the English invading Scotland three times (1544, 1545 and 1547). The Scots appealed to the French for help and the French agreed on one condition: that the infant Mary would be betrothed to the heir to the French throne. Thus Mary was sent to France and was married to Francis II.

In 1554 the Queen Mother, Mary de Guise, became the ruler of Scotland. She tolerated the Protestants, so Knox felt safe to return to Edinburgh. He preached fearlessly against corruption in the Church and against the papistry, and the authorities burnt his effigy as a warning.

IMAGE: Peering down a lane-way on the Royal Mile. Photograph: Miriam McWilliam

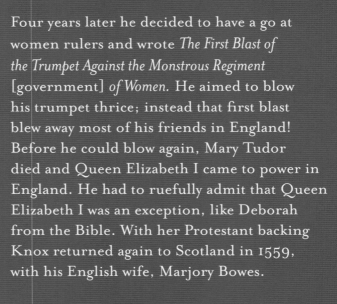

Four years later he decided to have a go at women rulers and wrote *The First Blast of the Trumpet Against the Monstrous Regiment* [government] *of Women.* He aimed to blow his trumpet thrice; instead that first blast blew away most of his friends in England! Before he could blow again, Mary Tudor died and Queen Elizabeth I came to power in England. He had to ruefully admit that Queen Elizabeth I was an exception, like Deborah from the Bible. With her Protestant backing Knox returned again to Scotland in 1559, with his English wife, Marjory Bowes.

Up until that time Knox had been known as a leading Reformer in England, and was even tainted with an English accent! It was the perfect time for him. Scottish Reformers had just nailed a 'Beggars Summons' on the door of the Scottish friaries telling them to surrender their properties and wealth to the poor.

In May 1559 Knox gave a series of fiery sermons in Perth. He preached against papistry, idolatry, tyranny and superstition, and promoted free speech and the gospel. It was said that: *'the voice of one man is able in one hour to put more life in us than five hundred trumpets continually blustering in our ears.'* [17]

People were so stirred up by his preaching that they surged forth, ransacking churches and destroying religious artworks, which were seen as idols. The movement gathered pace and Knox was brought to Edinburgh where he was installed as Minister of St Giles' in 1560.

That year the English made a treaty with the Scots against the French at Berwick and Mary de Guise died. The French were driven out and the Scottish people were left to settle their affairs.

Church leaders, together with dignitaries, sought to rebuild a new society for Scotland. Whilst St Giles' in the High Street was the preaching base of the Reformation, Magdalen Chapel in the Cowgate became the workshop for the transformation of our culture. This was the meeting place for the First General Assembly, and from here the blueprint for a Scottish culture built on Christian values, democratic Parliament, freedom of speech, education for all from primary school to university, issued forth to impact the world.[18]

It was here that the University of Edinburgh began with two Professors and a handful of students. John Knox and five other ministers were part of that group of 42 leaders that founded our modern culture. (This chapel was not only the birthplace of democratic Parliament, but also the birthplace of Presbyterianism and the building in which the first Methodist and Baptist churches in Edinburgh were founded. It was also used for preparing the bodies of the Covenant martyrs for burial.)

The huge assets of the Roman Catholic Church were seized (annual revenues in those days amounted to about £400,000, a huge amount!), which had been going to the rich bishops to maintain their lavish palaces, rather than to the poor and needy. Scotland also became free of papal dominion.

IMAGE: Statue of John Knox outside St Giles' Cathedral. Photograph: Miriam McWilliam

Despite Knox's loud protesting, the new government decided to split the money, with two thirds going to those already in possession of it, and one third being split between the Crown and the Reformed Church, to which Knox replied: *'two thirds (were) freely given to the devil, while the third must be divided between God and the devil'.*[19] He would have preferred it to go to developing education and social welfare, and the spreading of the gospel.

Finally, in 1572, John Knox was laid to rest in the graveyard behind St Giles' Cathedral. But you wouldn't know it! When I looked for his grave there I could not find it, so I asked the security guard who told me it is underneath car park lot No. 23. There is not even an inscription. This is how we remember John Knox today, the man who bravely stood up to Mary Queen of Scots and pioneered free speech and democracy! It was said of Mary Queen of Scots that she feared Knox's prayers more than the combined armies of France and Spain.

Let us instead give thanks to God for this prophet, who cried out to God *'Give me Scotland, or I die!'*, and remember him with the words of a notable historian:

> *'a quick survey of contemporary Scotsmen's opinion of John Knox would give us a picture of a ranting, vain, dogmatic misogynist. All four accusations are totally untrue... John Knox was a democrat. The ideal he gave Scotland as a legacy was of a democratic state, caring for its weakest members, with free education available to all, fiercely independent and with its own voice in Europe. Time will tell what we have done with that legacy.'*[20]

THE PRICE OF FREEDOM: THE COVENANTERS

John Barbour from the 14th century once said: *'Freedome is a noble thing.'* Usually it comes at a great price; such has often been the case in Scottish history. How true this was for this nation in the 17th century!

Exactly one hundred years to the very day after the six had been martyred by fire on Edinburgh's Castlehill, a document was signed by Christian leaders in Edinburgh called the *National Covenant* on 28th February, 1638. It was a long document, portions of which say the following:

'We all and every one of us under written protest, that after long and due examination of our own consciences in matters of true and false religion, are now thoroughly resolved in the truth by the Word and Spirit of God, and therefore we believe with our hearts, confess with our mouths, subscribe with our hands, and constantly affirm before God and the whole world, that this only is the true Christian faith and religion pleasing to God and bringing salvation to man, that is now by the mercy of God revealed to the world by the preaching of the blessed Gospel, and is now received, believed and defended by many and sundry notable kirks and realms, but chiefly by the kirk of Scotland, the King's majesty,

IMAGE: An inscription in Semple Close from 1638. This was the year of the signing of the National Covenant. Photograph: Miriam McWilliam

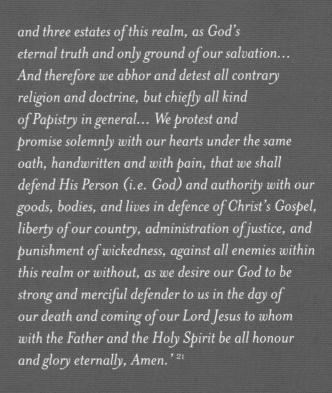

*and three estates of this realm, as God's
eternal truth and only ground of our salvation...
And therefore we abhor and detest all contrary
religion and doctrine, but chiefly all kind
of Papistry in general... We protest and
promise solemnly with our hearts under the same
oath, handwritten and with pain, that we shall
defend His Person (i.e. God) and authority with our
goods, bodies, and lives in defence of Christ's Gospel,
liberty of our country, administration of justice, and
punishment of wickedness, against all enemies within
this realm or without, as we desire our God to be
strong and merciful defender to us in the day of
our death and coming of our Lord Jesus to whom
with the Father and the Holy Spirit be all honour
and glory eternally, Amen.'* [21]

Much of the Covenant document lists the
errors of the Roman Catholic Church, such
as praying to the saints and angels and trusting
in our good works for eternal salvation, rather
than in Christ. As such, it shows a very real
concern that Scotland might be brought back
under papal tyranny and lose its freedom
gained through the Reformation. But how did
it come to this?

Charles I, supported by his Anglo-Catholic
Archbishop, William Laud, came up to
Scotland for his belated coronation, created a
hierarchy of bishops and turned St Giles' Kirk
into a cathedral. He also later issued a book of
canons reaffirming his own authority as Head
of the Scottish Church. The final straw was
when he forced the Scottish people to have an
Anglicised Prayer Book.

When it was read in St Giles' in 1637 a riot broke out, and in the following year the National Covenant was signed by Scottish leaders who were concerned that King Charles' policies were to bring back the nation to papal tyranny.

The Covenant was actually signed inside Greyfriars Kirk in the area of the Grassmarket by the barons and nobles. The following day it was signed by the clergy and merchants in the Tailors' Hall in the Cowgate, after which copies were signed in churches throughout Edinburgh and Scotland. In 1640 a Scottish Parliament met without authorisation of the King, and this was seen as open defiance and rebellion; this led to the outbreak of the Civil War between King Charles I and the Royalists, and the Parliamentarians led by Oliver Cromwell from England, who forged an alliance with the Scottish Covenanters.

After Charles I was executed, the Scots proclaimed Charles II as the new king and he was crowned at Scone after signing the National Covenants (there were two by now). This angered Cromwell who wanted no royal authority at all, even if it followed a Reformed position, and Civil War came to Scotland between Cromwell and the Covenanters. Charles II was enthroned in London and promptly forgot about his allegiance to the National Covenant, and decided that he would become the Head of the Church of Scotland.

IMAGE: Statue of Charles II in Parliament Square, behind St Giles' Cathedral. Photograph: Miriam McWilliam

He declared private gatherings ('Conventicles') of Christians unlawful and began persecuting the Church. From 1670 onwards any minister caught preaching in these gatherings would be executed. Thus began the 'Killing Times' in which over 18,000 Covenanters perished, over a hundred of them being executed here in Edinburgh. Some of them were executed for taking an armed stand for freedom of speech; most were murdered for simply practising their faith.

Many are the tales of the Covenanters. It was a brave but sad period of Scottish history. Often a Christian's only crime was to be at a prayer meeting or to be found with a Bible; regularly the soldiers shot them on the spot for these unlawful things. James White was caught at a prayer meeting near Kilmarnock and the soldiers shot him, then the Captain cut off his head with an axe and used his head as a makeshift 'football' on the grass.

In Wigton Bay Margaret Milliken and Margaret Wilson were tied with ropes and staked into the sand to be drowned by the incoming tide. In 1686 David Steel was caught at his farmhouse by soldiers who said he would have a fair trial. Instead they took him outside and blew off his head with their guns in front of his wife and child, and left his poor wife, Mary, to pick up the pieces of his head in a cloth. She cried out: *'The archers have shot at thee, my husband, but they could not reach thy soul; it has escaped like a dove far away, and is at rest.'* [22]

Archibald Campbell, Marquis of Argyll, was led to his execution by guillotine in the Edinburgh Grassmarket in 1661. On the scaffold he told the crowd: *'I had the honour to place the crown upon the king's brow; now he hastens me away to a better crown than his own.'* [23]

IMAGE: Above: Covenanters' Prison, Below: The Covenanters' Memorial Stone, in Greyfriars Kirk in the Grassmarket. Photographs: Paul James-Griffiths

Stooping to kiss the guillotine, which in those days was called 'The Maiden', he said: *'That's the sweetest maiden I've ever kissed!'* And then he was executed and his severed head impaled on a pole at Mercat Cross on the Royal Mile as a warning to others.

The Revd James Guthrie tried everything to bring about peace, but as he would not compromise his faith he was executed, and his head was driven onto a spike on the Netherbow Port (the city gates next to John Knox's House) and displayed there for 27 years. Often the Covenanters' hands and heads were placed there in a mock position of prayer.

John Wharry went cheerfully to his death. He put his head on the block but the executioner told him he wanted his right hand. Wharry called out: *'I am most willing to lay down my neck, hand and any other limbs of my body for the cause of Christ.'* [24]

After his hand had been cut off he held up his bloody stump to the crowd and shouted jubilantly: *'This blood now seals our Covenant!'*

The Revd Alexander Peden was regarded as a prophet and would often predict events accurately. He was continually hunted by the soldiers and tales of his escapes are legion. Sometimes he would use disguises, like wigs, or sometimes God would warn him of traps and so he would avoid being caught.

IMAGE: Place of public execution near St Giles'. Photograph: Miriam McWilliam

Miracles occurred at his open air meetings. He was leading a Conventicle in the Carrick Hills when soldiers came upon the believers. Suddenly from a clear sky a thick mist appeared from nowhere and surrounded the Covenanters so they could escape.

In his old age Peden often hid in a cave near Ochiltree and people sought him out for counsel and prayer; sometimes he would prophesy over them. He died of natural causes but the soldiers were so angry that he had died before execution that they dug him up after 40 days and buried him instead at the foot of a gallows tree.

Not all of the Covenanters lived peaceably. Many thought it was their duty to defend freedom of speech with arms and several battles ensued. The last one, the Battle of Bothwell Brig in 1679, was a great tragedy. They were defeated and the 1400 survivors were rounded up and taken to a makeshift prison next to Greyfriars Kirk, where the National Covenant had been signed. Crowded in what has been called the 'world's first concentration camp', many died of suffocation. The rest were either executed or sold into slavery, where most perished in a shipwreck.

Finally, in 1688, with the arrival of William of Orange, 'The Glorious Revolution' ensured the freedom of speech and religion that the Covenanters had longed for.

Today, if you visit the Grassmarket or Greyfriars Kirk, do pause for a minute by their monuments, and reflect on the Covenanters. Freedom is indeed a noble thing, and very costly.

IMAGE: The memorial for the Covenanter martyrs in the Grassmarket. Photograph: Miriam McWilliam

ATHENS OF THE NORTH: THE ENLIGHT- ENMENT

'Here I stand at what is called the [Mercat] Cross of Edinburgh, and can, in a few minutes, take fifty men of genius by the hand.' (Mr Amyat, the King's Chemist, 18th century)

The Reformation paved the way for enquiry, investigation and freedom of conscience and speech in Europe, out of which emerged great pioneer scientists, such as Kepler, Dalton, Newton, Pascal, Boyle, Ray, Herschel, Linnaeus, Euler and others, all of whom had a deep faith in the Creator and the Bible. But with this movement there also came freedom to enquire into alternative philosophies, and so humanism was born.

The original humanists, during and after the Reformation period, were usually radical Christian thinkers, but later humanism became associated with Deism (the belief that God started Creation but remained detached from it), and Atheism. A renaissance of ancient Greek philosophy took Europe by storm, and Edinburgh became known as the *Athens of the North*.

IMAGE: The Writers' Museum. Photograph: Miriam McWilliam

IMAGE: 'Hume' carved into stone. Photograph: Miriam McWilliam

DAVID HUME (1711–1776)

The father-figure of the Enlightenment Movement in Edinburgh was David Hume, a philosopher, historian and librarian. The execution of the first outspoken atheist, Thomas Aikenhead, a student from Edinburgh University in 1697, sowed seeds of discontent among many freethinkers. Coupled with this were the Church's sometimes very rigid and dour non-biblical rules that banned, for instance, bathing in a river on the Sabbath.

There was also a fresh wind of alternative philosophies blowing on the continent, especially in France, and so Hume went there in 1734, and spent much time discussing ideas with such men as Voltaire, Rousseau and Comte de Buffon. Whilst there he wrote his *Treatise of Human Nature* (1736), in which he sought to reintroduce the scientific methods of Newton and Francis Bacon without any need of a God. As an atheist he believed that the world came into being on its own and wrote in his *Treatise* and in the *Essays, Moral and Political:*

1. *All distinction betwixt virtue and vice is merely imaginary.*
2. *Justice has no foundation further than it contributes to public advantage.*
3. *Adultery is very lawful, but sometimes not expedient.*
4. *Religion and its ministers are prejudicial to mankind, and will always be found either to run into heights of superstition or enthusiasm.*
5. *Christianity has no evidence of its being a divine revelation.*
6. *Of all modes of Christianity Popery is the best, and the reformation from thence was only the work of madmen and enthusiasts.*[25]

Such statements were bound to provoke a reaction from church leaders and he appeared before the General Assembly in 1754 on the charge of heresy. Some of the ministers claimed he should be excommunicated from the Church, but as he was an atheist, such an idea was nonsense! He was eventually dismissed from the Assembly and left with some liberal clergy and friends to found *The Select Society*, which met in the original Advocates' Library off George IV Bridge. Everything could be discussed except for revealed religion, and this society led to many others being formed.

OTHER FAMOUS MEN OF THE ENLIGHTENMENT

There were dozens of men who influenced the world from Edinburgh with their ideas. **Adam Smith (1723–1790)**, was Hume's best friend and a Professor of Philosophy at Glasgow University. He settled in Panmure House in the Canongate part of the Royal Mile. He is best known as the political economist who changed the world through his book, *An Inquiry into the Nature and Causes of the Wealth of Nations* (1776). Indeed, his book became the 'Capitalists' Bible'.

Adam Ferguson (1723–1815) was a Professor of Philosophy at Edinburgh University and many regard him as the founder of evolutionary sociology.

IMAGE: Statue of David Hume, the father of the Scottish Enlightenment. Photograph: Miriam McWilliam

IMAGE: Above: The oldest Freemason Lodge building in the world today. The Lodges were the powerhouses for the Enlightenment. . Photograph: Miriam McWilliam

James Hutton (1726–1797) was a geologist who pioneered uniformitarianism (the belief that the rocks were formed gradually over vast periods of time, rather than being laid down during the Creation and the biblical Flood). Charles Lyell, another Scotsman, developed his work and made it popular in 1830. William Cullen (1710–1790) was a Professor of Medicine at Edinburgh University and under his direction the University became the most advanced medical college in the world at that time.

Dugald Stewart (1753–1828) held the chair at Edinburgh University for Moral Philosophy. He gave Edinburgh the name *Athens of the North,* because much of the Enlightenment was based upon the philosophy of the ancient Athenian Greeks, such as Plato, Aristotle, Socrates and Epicurus. Some scholars even consider that Adam Smith's economic theory was based upon that of Xenophon from Athens.

William Smellie (1740–1790) pioneered a printing house in Anchor Close, just off the Royal Mile, and produced the many philosophical and scientific tomes of the Enlightenment Movement. He edited and printed the first *Encyclopaedia Britannica,* as well as Buffon's *Natural History.* He also anticipated the ideas of Freud and Jung in his book, *On Dreams.*

FREEMASON LODGES: POWERHOUSES OF THE ENLIGHTENMENT

The oldest existing Freemason Lodge building in the world is on St John's Street, off the Royal Mile. As in France, Edinburgh's Freemason Lodges opened up their doors to spread the Enlightenment. Most of the key men from the Movement were Freemasons, such as

Lord Kames, Lord Hailes, Lord Monboddo, Dugald Stewart, Sir Walter Scott and Robert Burns. Freemasonry has its modern roots in Scotland. The first record of Freemason Lodges is in 1598 when the King of Scotland commissioned William Schaw to establish them in a more organisational way, and Sir Francis Bacon gave spiritual insight.

Although Masonic Lodges might appear to be 'Christian', they are not; the spiritual roots are derived from ancient pagan mystery rites and Gnosticism, overlaid with Christian symbolism, with which Bacon was very familiar. Some people claim that Freemasonry evolved through a mixture of the Knights Templar, Rosicrucianism and Merchant Societies.

Much excitement has surrounded Rosslyn Chapel, built in 1446 by William Sinclair, allegedly a member of the Knights Templar. This chapel, situated only seven miles from Edinburgh, featured in the Dan Brown fantasy-fiction *The Da Vinci Code*.

During the Enlightenment Movement the Freemason John Robison, a Professor of Natural Philosophy at Edinburgh University published a volume entitled *Proofs of a Conspiracy* (1798), in which he exposed *The Illuminati*. Professor Adam Weishaupt of Germany had founded this Order on 1st May, 1776, which heavily infiltrated Freemasonry in Europe.

IMAGE: Medusa's head on the back of David Hume's statue. This was the symbol of Athena, patron goddess of the arts and science. Photograph: Miriam McWilliam

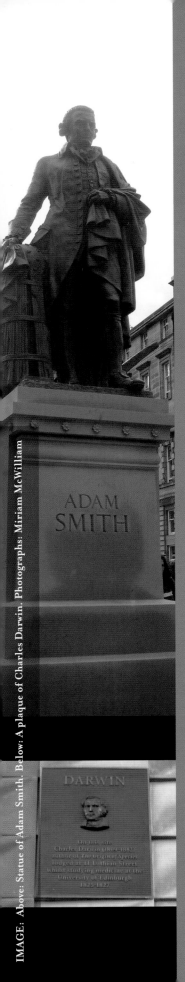

It had as its goal the removal of Christianity, nationalism, royalty, privatism and the family unit, and sought to replace it with communistic ideals based on the occult. Robison's book caused a sensation across Europe, as he claimed this secret Order was responsible for the French Revolution and had plans for world revolution and dominance.[26]

THE RISE OF EVOLUTION

Usually people think of the Theory of Evolution as an idea discovered by Charles Darwin and made widely known through his book, *The Origin of Species* (1859). However, the idea had been growing in pace in Europe over a hundred years before him, and had its roots in the Greek philosophers centuries before Christ, and even in Hindu Vedantic philosophy long before that.[27]

Ancient Greek philosophy became fashionable in the Enlightenment period and so naturalistic explanations of the universe also became popular with many philosophers such as Hume (*Dialogues Concerning Natural Religion*, 1776), Comte de Buffon, Lamarck and Laplace.

James Burnett (Lord Monboddo; 1714– 1799) a High Court Judge, Freemason and anthropologist from Edinburgh was obsessed with the ancient Greeks, and he used to run round his house and garden naked and have cold baths in all weathers.

Back in 1768 he was convinced that humans had evolved through a process of God-given natural laws from vegetation through to animals, and thence to orang-utans, and finally people.[28]

IMAGE: Above: Statue of Adam Smith. Below: A plaque of Charles Darwin. Photographs: Miriam McWilliam

Lord Neaves of Edinburgh, another High Court Judge, penned the Scottish opinion about the true founder of Evolution in 1875 with the words:

> *'Though Darwin now proclaims the law*
> *And spreads it far abroad, O!*
> *The man that first the secret saw*
> *Was honest old Monboddo.*
> *The architect precedence takes*
> *Of him that bears the hod, O!*
> *So up and at them, Land of Cakes,*
> *We'll vindicate Monboddo.'*

Monboddo was, however, a religious person and argued with the atheists of the time. He claims that a beautiful woman appeared to him in a fever, and spoke to him in French about a philosophy that merged together the ideas of Aristotle, Newton and Evolution. In the preface of his mammoth work, *Antient Metaphysics,* he shows us the roots of his evolutionary thinking in Aristotle, Plato, Pythagoras and the Egyptian religion.

ERASMUS DARWIN AND HIS GRANDSON CHARLES

Charles Darwin's grandfather, Erasmus Darwin, studied medicine at Edinburgh University (1753–1754) and was a Freemason and philosopher. Influenced by Monboddo he wrote *Zoonomia, Or the Laws of Organic Life* in 1803, in which he proposed an evolutionary model, and *The Temple of Nature,* a poem based

IMAGE: An Edinburgh sunset. Photograph: Miriam McWilliam

on the pagan mystery religions, through which he also expounded the doctrine of Evolution. Hence, Charles Darwin, who also studied medicine at Edinburgh University, came from a line of evolutionary philosophers, and he naturally imbibed those ideas here before writing his famous book in 1859.

THE CHURCH'S REACTION TO THE ENLIGHTENMENT

Not surprisingly such a movement challenged the very existence of the Church in Europe and Edinburgh. It was rent asunder by a division between the *Moderates* and the *High Flyers*. The High Flyers were those in the Church who held on to traditional Christianity, and the Moderates were those who either became very liberal in their Christian understanding of biblical truth, or who held to a biblical position but sought to challenge the very strict religious straitjacket of the age.

Some of the clergy, led by the example of Rev. Professor William Robertson, Principal of Edinburgh University, who stated that *'miracles are now ceased'*, followed the fashion of the day and frequented the Enlightenment's many philosophical societies, trying to compromise and become accepted. For them, quoting from Scripture from the pulpit seemed like heresy, whereas the philosophers were embraced with relish – much to the bewilderment of their parishioners! Into this confusion fell a mass of ordinary people, who, with absolute truth removed, shook off 'Bible morality'.

According to contemporary statistics, divorce and separation dramatically increased, brothels multiplied by twenty times and the number of

IMAGE: A stained glass window, St Giles' Cathedral. Photograph: Miriam McWilliam

street prostitutes by one hundred times, and theft, house-breaking and crime sky-rocketed.[29]

Into this scene came Christians who preached and lived biblical morality but who shrugged off the Deism and Atheism of the humanists on the one hand, and the rigid regime of the High-Flyer clergy on the other. Even back in 1729, Rev. Robert Wallace had argued: *'We live in an Age so enlightened when weak arguments and bad reasonings will not pass so well as formerly.'* [30] He called for intellectual Christians who would use their minds for God, and sought to promote science and the arts.

GEORGE WHITEFIELD AND JOHN WESLEY IN EDINBURGH

The Revd Alexander Webster decided to invite the Methodist preacher, George Whitefield, to Edinburgh. He came and preached 14 times (1741–1756) and shook the city with his message. It has been estimated that crowds of up to 20,000 (half the city then) gathered to hear him preach in Parliament Square, outside St Giles. Multitudes were converted and transformed.

John Wesley also came in this period and preached 22 times here (between 1751 and 1790), having a great effect on the populace.

IMAGE: An inscription encouraging Christian unity, 1677. Photograph: Miriam McWilliam

IMAGE: 1. David Nasmith. 2. Coffee outreach in 1910. 3. ECM open air outreach. 4. ECM helping the poor. Photograph: Miriam McWilliam

He said that the only danger he had was of being hugged to death by the grateful citizens of Edinburgh! Once, though, he had just been preaching up by the Castle, when two policemen arrested him on a charge of kidnapping someone! The confusion was cleared up and Wesley was set free from the Tolbooth Prison on the Royal Mile, and the slanderer was fined £1,000 (£400 Scottish) — a tidy sum in those days!

THE GREAT AWAKENING: THE 19TH CENTURY

SOCIAL REFORM

The atheist Edinburgh student, Aikenhead, had said that Christianity would be *'extirpated'* (destroyed) by 1800, but contrary to his prediction, the Church experienced a phenomenal surge and growth in the 19th century.

Part of the fruit of the Enlightenment Movement had been its impact on the clergy, many of whom were now more interested in philosophy, gambling, drinking and the theatre, than looking after the poor and needy. A growing number of devout Christians determined to do something about it.

In 1874 Lord Shaftesbury spoke publicly of **David Nasmith (1799-1839)** *'of whom all Scotsmen may well boast'*. Why was this? After all, most people have never even heard of him!

Nasmith was born and brought up in Glasgow and founded over sixty Christian societies in his dynamic, but short life. He is particularly remembered for pioneering the YMCA and City Missions.

In 1832 he came to this city and set up the Edinburgh City Mission in a shop at 375 High St (Royal Mile), opposite St Giles' Cathedral. He preached that the cities of Britain needed their own missionaries who had experienced life in normal jobs, and not just in theological colleges. He also preached that all true Christians from across the Church denominations should work together to get the job done of transforming their communities.

Many ministers in the Church at the time sneered at his impudence and enthusiasm, thinking that what he had proposed was impossible and preposterous! Not put off by their attitude, he gathered together ministers who had a real heart for God and people, and set about commissioning men and women in the city to transform the darkest slums into places of heaven.

Just seven years later Edinburgh City Mission (ECM) was so effective in its work that '*a missionary spirit*' had been released in the city. In 1841 many prostitutes, criminals and drunkards in the Grassmarket were dramatically changed through the preaching of these missionaries.

IMAGE: A stained glass window, St Giles' Cathedral. Photograph: Miriam McWilliam

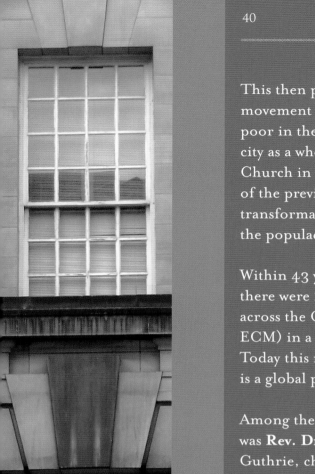

IMAGE: Bagpiper on the Royal Mile. Photograph: Miriam McWilliam

This then prepared the way for a larger movement in 1859 that deeply impacted the poor in the Royal Mile area, and indeed the city as a whole. The huge ingathering into the Church in the 1873 Revival was an accumulation of the previous waves, and led to an astounding transformation of the city in every section of the populace.

Within 43 years from Nasmith setting up ECM there were 130 missionaries working together across the Church denominations (33 were in ECM) in a deeply holistic, Christ-centred way. Today this model of inter-church mission work is a global phenomenon.

Among the leading Christian activists of the day was **Rev. Dr Thomas Guthrie (1792–1873)**. Guthrie, challenged by the courageous work of ECM, investigated the plight of the poor in Edinburgh. He was shocked by the bad behaviour of the children who were left to roam the streets in wild, filthy gangs. He wrote:

> *'I wandered... whole days without ever seeing a Bible, or indeed any book at all. I often stood in rooms bare of any furniture; where father, mother, and half a dozen children had neither bed nor bedding, unless a heap of straw and dirty rags huddled in a corner could be called so. I have heard the wail of children crying for bread, and their mother had none to give them... I have known a father turn his step-daughter to the street at night... bidding the sobbing girl who bloomed into womanhood, earn her bread there as others were doing. I have bent over the foul pallet of a dying lad to hear him whisper how his father and mother... who were sitting half-drunk by the fireside... had pulled the blankets off his body to sell them for drink. I have seen children whitened like plants growing in a cellar... when they cry they are not kissed*

*but beaten... I don't recollect of ever
seeing a mother in these wretched dwellings
bouncing her infant, or hearing the little
creature crow or laugh as he leapt for joy.
There, infants have no toys; and their
mothers' smiles are as rare as sunshine.'* [31]

Throughout his life he was a champion
for the poor, stirring up the Church
and the government. His loud cry was:
*'Do it now! It is not safe to leave a generous
feeling to the cooling influences of the world.'*

Working together with the churches and
the Edinburgh City Mission, Guthrie
pioneered the *Ragged Schools* for the
poor children, in which they learnt to
read and write and were educated not
just in Scripture, but other subjects
too, besides having food, clothing and
medical care provided. The first school
was near the Castle off the Royal Mile
at St Columba's Free Church (formerly
Free St John's), where Guthrie was the
minister. These schools multiplied and
eventually became part of the foundation
for the State Education System.

**Rev. Professor Thomas Chalmers
(1780–1847)** was also a great pioneer
in education and social welfare. William
Wilberforce, the great English social
reformer, said about him: *'all the world is
wild about Dr. Chalmers'.*

Not only did Chalmers become
Principal of New College in Edinburgh
but he also developed a model in his
parish of St John's (1820s) that had a
huge influence on the social welfare
system of today.

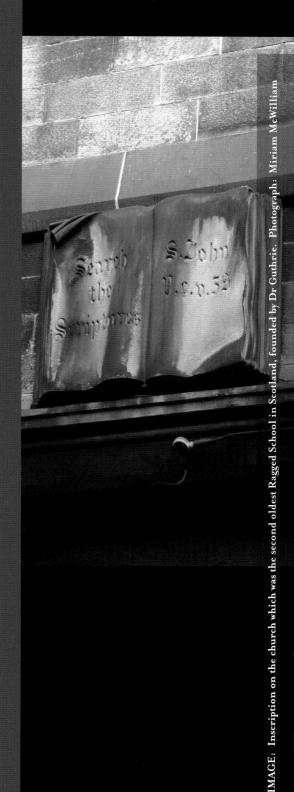

IMAGE: Inscription on the church which was the second oldest Ragged School in Scotland, founded by Dr Guthrie. Photograph: Miriam McWilliam

IMAGE: The Hub, the Royal Mile. Photograph: Miriam McWilliam

He was the first person to challenge, in book form, the capitalism of Adam Smith's *Wealth of Nations* with his works *The Christian and Civic Economy of Large Towns* (1826) and *Political Economy* (1832).

He also became the first Moderator of the Free Church of Scotland in 1843 when there was a huge split in the Church. The reason for *'The Disruption'*, as it was called, was government interference in appointing clergy in the Church. The cry of 'Freedom!' led to 470 ministers storming out of the Assembly and setting up their own Free Church, with Chalmers as the leader.

Medical and Scientific Discoveries

Edinburgh University was a leading world centre in the sciences, particularly in medicine. Amongst the famous pioneers of science in this period were several Christians. **Thomas Young (1773–1829)** studied at Edinburgh University where he also became a Professor of Medicine. He invented the double-slit experiment for studying light.

Sir David Brewster (1781–1868) was Principal at Edinburgh University and edited the scientific part of the *Edinburgh Encyclopaedia*; he was also instrumental in founding the *British Association for the Advancement of Science*. He invented the kaleidoscope and refined the science of microscopes, and discovered what became known as *'Brewster's Law'*, which became the forerunner of laser technology.

As a dedicated Christian and Fellow of the Royal Society, he said: *'It can't be presumption to be SURE (of our forgiveness) because it is Christ's work, not ours; on the contrary, it is presumption to doubt His word and work.'* [32]

On his death bed he said: *'I shall see Jesus, and that will be grand. I shall see him who made the worlds.'*

Sir James Young Simpson (1811–1870) trained as an obstetrician and became a Professor of Midwifery at Edinburgh University. He pioneered the medical use of chloroform and administered this to Queen Victoria for the birth of her son, Prince Leopold, in 1847. He was a very dedicated Christian who led the Medical Dispensary work for the poor at Carrubbers Close Mission on the Royal Mile. When asked what was his greatest discovery, he cheerfully replied that it was finding Christ as his Saviour.

Lord Joseph Lister (1827–1912) went to study medicine at Edinburgh University under Professor James Syme, a Christian who was also regarded as one of the world's best surgeons of that period. In 1869 Lister became Professor of Clinical Surgery at Edinburgh University and he discovered antiseptics and hugely advanced surgical methods.

IMAGE: A stained glass window in St Giles' Cathedral Photograph: Miriam McWilliam

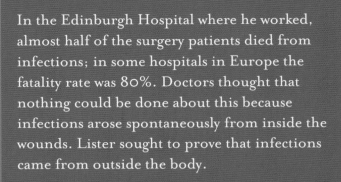

In the Edinburgh Hospital where he worked, almost half of the surgery patients died from infections; in some hospitals in Europe the fatality rate was 80%. Doctors thought that nothing could be done about this because infections arose spontaneously from inside the wounds. Lister sought to prove that infections came from outside the body.

He came across the work done by the Frenchman, Louis Pasteur (1860), whose experiments proved that germs were airborne and not inherent in the body. He showed that by sealing off the air we could block out germs. This destroyed the theory of spontaneous generation (a forerunner of Evolution), popular since Aristotle's time. This then encouraged Lister to experiment, and he discovered that carbolic acid killed off the germs on the human body without harming the patient. Thus, antiseptics were pioneered.

Lord Lister was outspoken about his faith. He said: *'I am a believer in the fundamental doctrines of Christianity.'* [33]

James Clerk Maxwell (1831–1879), alongside Newton and Einstein, has been regarded as one of the greatest scientists of all time. He was born here and went to Edinburgh University. Whilst he was Professor of Experimental Physics at Cambridge University he planned and constructed the Cavendish physics laboratory. He is famous for formulating and establishing a unified theory of physics that pulled together light, electricity and magnetism. His work paved the way for Einstein's theory of relativity, radio, television, radar, satellite communication and x-ray.

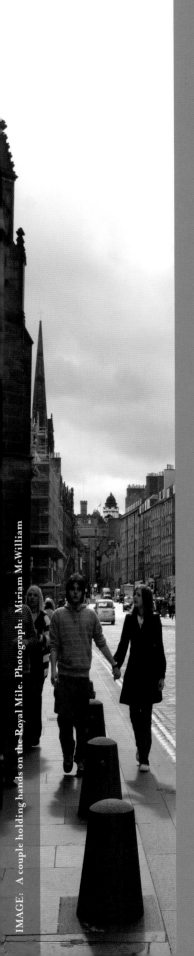

IMAGE:: A couple holding hands on the Royal Mile. Photograph: Miriam McWilliam

He was a dedicated Christian and outspoken advocate against naturalistic evolution. He destroyed Laplace's *'Nebular Hypothesis'* (1796), which promoted the idea that the universe spontaneously evolved out of a gas cloud. He also presented a paper to the British Association for the Advancement of Science (1873), in which he said:

> *'No theory of evolution can be formed to account for the similarity of molecules, for evolution necessarily implies continuous change... the exact equality of each molecule to all others of the same kind gives it... the essential character of a manufactured article, and precludes the idea of its being eternal and self existent.'* [34]

He wrote this prayer:

> *'Almighty God, Who has created man in Thine own image, and made him a living soul that he might seek after Thee, and have dominion over Thy creatures, teach us to study the works of Thy hands, that we may subdue the earth to our use, and strengthen the reason for Thy service; so to receive Thy blessed Word, that we may believe on Him Whom Thou has sent, to give us the knowledge of salvation and the remission of our sins. All of which we ask in the name of the same Jesus Christ, our Lord.'* [35]

IMAGE: Prayer candles and a stained glass window in St Giles' Cathedral. Photograph: Miriam McWilliam

IMAGE: Gateway at the end of the Royal Mile. Photograph: Miriam McWilliam

THE 1859 REVIVAL

Charles Finney, the noted American evangelist, visited Edinburgh in 1859 and preached to a crowded church gathering throughout the week, but was discouraged by the lack of results and left a day early. A headmaster from Pilrig School (Leith), William Robertson, went every night seeking to know Christ for himself, but came away disappointed. Finally, on the last night, he truly experienced Christ for himself, but through a Dr Kirk, and not the famous evangelist.

Robertson, full of joy, taught at Pilrig School the next week and something supernatural started happening. One child after another began openly weeping and grieving over the bad things they had done until the school itself went into mourning. The Christian teachers there suddenly found themselves in the middle of a revival, in which God supernaturally visits people in an extraordinary way. The children's mourning was turned into great rejoicing as they found forgiveness and eternal life through Christ. Their transformed lives led to teachers and parents becoming Christians, and the movement spread through the community.

Robertson was asked to hold meetings at Carrubbers Close Mission in the Royal Mile, which had been re-consecrated as a Christian building in 1858, after the atheist club, *The Celebrated Cathedral of the Prince of Darkness,* had closed down. Crowds were drawn without advertising, as if they were pins being irresistibly pulled to a huge magnet.

A contemporary report says:

'Night after night the careless became earnest, the earnest became convicted, and the convicted at length found peace in the blood of Jesus.' [36]

The gatherings became so large that the Mission could not contain the numbers, and hundreds of desperate people were turned away. They ended up meeting for a while in the Theatre Royal and *'a rich harvest of souls was reaped at every meeting, and cases of the most thrilling and engrossing interest were continually occurring'.* [37]

Everywhere in the city there was talk about God's visit to Edinburgh. Daily packed prayer meetings took place in the Tron Kirk on the Royal Mile, and crowds of up to 10,000 would turn up to hear gospel preaching in places like Queen's Park, Grassmarket, Parliament Square and Calton Hill. The most remarkable thing about this movement was the way in which the children, the marginalised, the poor, the criminals and alcoholics were totally transformed. In Newhaven (the port in North Edinburgh) this was especially the case for *'things of eternity seemed to press upon the community, so that nothing short of salvation would satisfy the people.'* [38]

Out of this significant revival came hundreds of eager missionaries who gladly gave their lives for Christ and his cause in places like Africa and Asia, spreading a holistic and life-changing message, accompanied by a

IMAGE: Contemporary architecture on the Royal Mile today. Photograph: Miriam McWilliam

host of hospitals, schools and other good works that sprouted up everywhere they went. Today millions of ordinary people in those countries give thanks to God for that costly work, for many of those missionaries died through disease or even through martyrdom.

David Livingstone (1813–1873), from an earlier period, had established the Church in parts of Africa. Although he was from Glasgow, he studied medicine at Edinburgh University. His statue exists in Princes Gardens where he holds out his Bible to the passers-by.

Eric Liddell, made memorable by the film *Chariots of Fire,* was an Olympic gold medallist (1924), who studied at Edinburgh University, and who died for his faith as a missionary in the Far East. It was said that *'all Scotland mourned his death'.*

MOODY AND SANKEY

In 1873 two Americans hit Edinburgh like a whirlwind: Sankey charmed the people with his spiritual singing, and Moody electrified them with his preaching. It was said by the hymn-writer, Rev. Dr Horatius Bonar, that almost every home in Edinburgh had been affected by the visit.

The queues of people waiting to get a place at the meetings stretched from the Assembly Hall (The Mound) to Princes Street. The tour was so effective that by the end the only place big enough for the crowds was the field below Arthur's Seat, at the bottom of the Royal Mile.

Moody and Sankey came across the work of the Carrubbers Close Mission in the Royal Mile and were so impressed that they decided to raise funds for a new building. They had the novel idea of raising money in a horse-drawn cart that slowly moved down the entire length of the Royal Mile. Whilst Sankey sang and Moody preached, people threw money into the buckets. Eventually, after more fundraising, a new building was established and in 1884 was consecrated. Today it is known as Carrubbers Christian Centre.

The First World Missionary Conference (1910)

In 1910 an extraordinary meeting took place in Edinburgh. It was billed as *The World Missionary Conference*. The slogan of the week was *'Evangelising the world in our generation'*. Missionaries poured in from 120 countries around the globe in what was the first world missionary conference. Sadly, after being stirred by that week, the vision was largely drowned by two World Wars in Europe.

IMAGE: Psalms and poetry engraved on Parliament House. Photograph: Miriam McWilliam

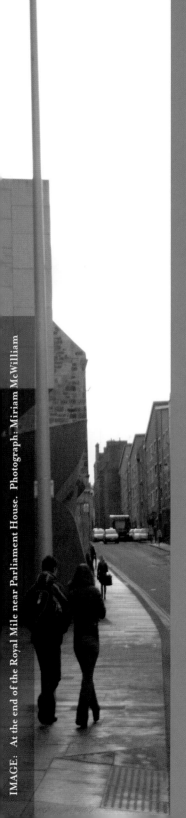

EDINBURGH TODAY: THE 21ST CENTURY

Today's Edinburgh would be a shock to previous generations of Christians who laboured for Christ and gave their blood for Scotland's freedom. The current spiritual climate is either atheistic and secular, or increasingly pagan. Humanistic evolution has crippled the life of the Church, and those who are spiritually searching are mostly looking for answers in New Age ideas.

The old Celtic gods have returned and about 12,000 people annually go up to Calton Hill to celebrate *Beltane*, Europe's biggest pagan festival, and another pagan festival, *Samhuinn (Samhain)* is celebrated on the Royal Mile. At least seven ghost and witchcraft tours exist on the Royal Mile, attracting many thousands of people every year. There is even now an annual Ghost Festival.

Indeed, there is a concerted effort to turn Edinburgh into *'The Paranormal Capital of Europe'*, and others boast that Edinburgh is the most haunted city in the world. No doubt this is being fuelled by the fact that the present street of the Royal Mile lies on top of an underground 'city', which had been sealed up in the seventeenth century to prevent the plague from spreading. But the witches also have their martyrs in Scotland from the *'Burning Times'*, in which thousands of them were killed, although most were just ordinary people, even Christians.

Edinburgh has a long, adventurous and mystical past which has inspired many authors, such as J. M. Barrie *(Peter Pan)*, the spiritualist, Arthur Conan Doyle *(Sherlock Holmes books)*, and Robert

Louis Stevenson (*Treasure Island, Kidnapped* and *Dr Jekyll and Mr Hyde*). The supernatural is now a big business, with J. K. Rowling's *Harry Potter* books making her one of the world's richest women, and Dan Brown's *The Da Vinci Code*, which features Rosslyn Chapel outside Edinburgh, making him a multi-millionaire.

Now Edinburgh is a world centre for the Arts and Science. It is a city on the pulse of a world paradigm shift. In the heart of this amazing city stands St Giles' Cathedral, a symbol of the resurrection power of Christ. The Church has been this way before, and just when people have written it off, God breathes his resurrection power into it to transform our culture. And none more so in history than Edinburgh. There is hope. Something is stirring once more, like a dormant volcano coming back to life.

Today God is just as real to many people here in Edinburgh. Let's hear from some of the locals about what God has done in their lives:

'I was a chronic alcoholic and was homeless... then I asked Jesus into my life. He has changed my life beyond measure. I have been sober for 17 years, married for 18 years, and now I'm working as Director of Residential Support Services with Bethany Christian Trust, helping homeless and vulnerable people. I am now able to pass on the love of Christ

IMAGE: Scottish Parliament building. Photograph: Miriam McWilliam

to others in a very practical outworking of my faith, and have experienced the joy of seeing others set free through his love.'

(John Rodgers, Director of Residential Support Services)

'Before I became a Christian I felt that something was missing, as though I had a big hole inside me. I had a good life, good job, good husband and no particular problems but everything seemed empty and meaningless. I can truthfully say that since I became a Christian I feel fulfilled, secure and loved. Over the years I have had many answers to prayer that have astounded me, and I know that God loves me and is concerned about everything and everyone I am concerned about.'

(Sylvia Rebus, Personal Assistant)

'When I was very young I went to church, but I thought God was just a human invention to make kids behave. As I grew up I believed in Evolution and the Big Bang. Whilst at university I argued with my Christian flatmates, all of whom were scientists. I was convinced that the Bible had been disproved through science, but they showed me the unfounded assumptions my science was based on. After reading the New Testament I knew God was real and that I had broken his laws and was not fit for heaven and that if I died he would rightly send me to hell. I asked for his forgiveness, knowing that Jesus had died on the cross so I could receive this, and I believed that he had risen from the dead. I now know that when I die I will be in heaven; this is a supernatural assurance and it frees me to live the rest of my life without worrying about the future. Living in the light of heaven has transformed my life on earth.'

(Phil Holden, Freelance Web Designer)

IMAGE: Contemporary architecture at Parliament House. Photograph: Miriam McWilliam

View our website: theroyalmile.org.uk

For further help, or to receive a
FREE GOSPEL OF JOHN, which also
explains how you can have a personal
relationship with God, please contact:

Edinburgh City Mission
Nasmith House, 9 Pilrig St.
Edinburgh EH6 5AH,
Ph: 0131 554 6140
Email: info@ecm.org

The Celtic Tour also runs in
Edinburgh, which is a dramatic re-
telling of the spiritual history of the
Royal Mile through acting, stories and
song. Details of this tour and subjects
related to this booklet can be found
on their website at www.celtictour.org.
Bookings can be taken from Edinburgh
City Mission (details above).

Courses available to discover more
about the Christian faith can be
found at:

THE ALPHA COURSE

Over 11 million people have been
on this course, which lasts ten weeks.
It has been recommended by all of
the major church denominations. For
details contact their website at alpha.org

CHRISTIANITY EXPLORED

This alternative course is based on
Mark's Gospel and is recommended.
For details, contact their website at
www.christianityexplored.com

IMAGE: Holyrood Palace. Photograph: Miriam McWilliam

IMAGE: Old Fishmarket Close. Photograph: Miriam McWilliam

NOTES

1   Tertullian, *Def. Fides*, p. 179.
2   Lee, F.N., *Sixth Century Christian Britain from King Arthur to Rome's Augustine*, p. 2, www.dr-fnlee.org/docs4/arthur/arthur.pdf.
3   Adomnan of Iona, *Life of St Columba*, 2:32, p. 179–80, Penguin Classics © 1995.
4   Ibid., 2:34, p. 182–84.
5   Bede, *Life of Cuthbert*, Introduction, p. 41, Penguin Classics © 1965.
6   Ibid., chapter 32, p. 83-4.
7   Ibid., chapter 22, p. 71.
8   Ibid., chapter 7, p. 52.
9   Ibid., chapter 17, p. 66.
10 Ibid., chapter 22, p. 71.
11 It is unlikely that the present Stone of Destiny is the original. Some historians think that the original stone was moved from Scone by the monks who anticipated that the English would steal it. Its present place of resting remains a mystery.
12 Knox, John, *The Reformation in Scotland*, p. 6, Banner of Truth © 2000.
13 Ibid., p. 8.
14 Ibid., p. 37.
15 Donaldson, Gordon, *John Knox: Scotland's Great Reformer*, p. 3–4, Pitkin © 2000.
16 Ibid., p. 6.
17 Ibid., p. 15.
18 The Magdalen Chapel Museum and leaflet.
19 Donaldson, Gordon, *John Knox*, p. 17.
20 Graham, Roderick, *John Knox: Democrat*, p. 12 and 354, Robert Hale Ltd. © 2001.
21 Steele, Alan J., *The National Covenant in its Historical Setting*, p. 14–17, © 2003, published by the Society of Friends of the Kirk of the Greyfriars.

22 Love, Dane, *Scottish Covenanter Stories: Tales from the Killing Times*, p. 221, Neil Wilson Publishing © 2005.

23 Ibid., p. 2.

24 Ibid., p. 99–100.

25 Buchan, James, *Capital of the Mind: How Edinburgh Changed the World*, p. 99, John Murray Publishers © 2003.

26 Stauffer, Vernon, *New England and the Bavarian Illuminati*, Chapter III, p. 14–42, www.conspiracyarchive.com/NWO/Stauffer_Illuminati.htm.

27 Barnes, Jonathan, *Early Greek Philosophy*, Penguin Classics © 1987. Many of the Greek philosophers sought to explain the existence of the universe through naturalistic means. For example, Anaximander (610–540 BC) had a 'Big Bang' hypothesis (p. 72, 73), and taught that humans came from fish (p. 72). One earlier Hindu Vedantic version (c. 1400 BC) of this suggests that the 'Big Bang' occurred by itself about 4.32 billion years ago, and that the earth cooled down and life came from the water and went through various stages of evolution right up to white-skinned man (Brahmin). They favoured an eternal universe theory of course, with 'Big Bangs' and 'Big Crunches' continuing in an endless cycle — a theory that may come back into fashion again today.

IMAGE: Canongate Kirk. Photograph: Paul James-Griffiths

28 From the preface (xvii-xviii) of a copy of
    James Burnett's book *An Account of a Savage
    Girl, Caught Wild in the Woods of Champagne*, cited
    by James Buchan in his *Capital of the Mind*,
    p. 234–235, and from Burnett's *Of the Origin
    and Progress of Language*, 1773, p. 174–175, cited
    by Buchan in *Capital of the Mind*, p. 235.

29 *Capital of the Mind*, p. 320.

30 Ibid., p. 66.

31 From the Christian History Institute,
    quoted from Celtic Christian Tour:
    Historical Notes, p. 74.

32 Graves, Dan, *Scientists of Faith*, p. 95,
    Kregel Resources © 1996.

33 Lamont, Anne, *21 Great Scientists who Believed
    the Bible*, p. 196, Creation Science
    Foundation © 1995.

34 Ibid., p. 207.

35 Ibid., p. 208.

36 *1858 – 1909: These Fifty Years:
    The Story of Carrubbers Close Mission
    Edinburgh*, p. 21, The Tract and
    Colportage Society of Scotland, 1909.

37 Ibid., p. 22.

38 Ibid., p. 71.

ACKNOWLEDGEMENTS

Many thanks to the following for helping with this publication: Alison and Stephen Carter for their unswerving support and generosity; Miriam McWilliam for her design and encouragement; Dr Patricia Meldrum, Dr Neil Macdonald, Bill Anderson and Cameron Rose for historical advice, and for Phil Holden and a host of others that have upheld me during the whole process.

Edinburgh city motto since 1647: *Nisi Dominus Frustra* 'Except the Lord in vain'. Taken from Psalm 127 (Authorised Version):

'Except the Lord build the house
They labour in vain that build it:
Except the Lord keep the city
The watchmen waketh but in vain.'

IMAGE: Edinburgh Castle. Photograph: Miriam McWilliam

IMAGE: The Royal Mile. Photograph: Miriam McWilliam

IMAGE: A stained glass window in St Giles' Cathedral. Photograph : Miriam McWilliam